Gluten-Free Vegan Cookbook

Plant-Based & Clean Eating Dairy Free Recipes to Reduce Gluten Intolerance Symptoms

By Kira Novac (ISBN-13:9781532795039)

www.amazon.com/author/kira-novac

Free Complimentary Recipe eBook

Thank you so much for taking an interest in my work!

As a thank you, I would love to offer you a free complimentary recipe eBook to help you achieve vibrant health. It will teach you how to prepare amazingly tasty and healthy gluten-free treats so that you never feel deprived or bored again!

As a special bonus, you will be able to receive all my future books (kindle format) for free or only $0.99.

Download your free recipe eBook here:

http://bit.ly/gluten-free-desserts-book

Table of contents

About This Book

The Spiralizer is a revolutionary device that is a great addition to any healthy kitchen. This nifty gadget, with its different settings that form your fruits and vegetables into a variety of different shapes and sizes, allows you to create healthy, filling and very tasty meals that are guaranteed to be nutritious and just plain good for you. More and more society is looking at healthier ways of living and eating. The vegan and gluten-free approach to your diet has many benefits to both those who chose a completely vegan way of life and those who are looking to base their overall diets on sound nutrition.

Everyone loves a comforting bowl of pasta or a curry with rice, but the high gluten content of such grains often leaves one feeling heavy and bloated, not to mention they are high in calories that will only be necessary if you are about to enter a triathlon.

Furthermore, with the increased global population, many farming methods have had to become ones that focus on quantity of crops as opposed to quality, thus resulting in many people having compromised immune systems and a rise in food allergies and many types of cancer.

A vegan, gluten-free approach to your diet can help you control this, and the Spiralizer device makes it even easier. By including organically grown fresh vegetables, fruits, beans and pulses, seeds, herbs, healthy fats and some super foods, the recipes in this book will give you all the inspiration you need, and since they are so easy to prepare, there's no excuse to start Spiralizing today.

The Spiralizer device is available in most home and kitchen supply stores, and can also be bought online. Almost any vegetable or fruit can be Spiralized, so the variety is endless!

The spiralizer brand I recommend is *Yanu*® (you can get their spiralizer from Amazon.com or from YanuKitchen.com). They have excellent customer service, and as an added bonus, they will send you 8 free recipe eBooks with your spiralizer.

This book is divided into three sections to give you an abundance of Spiralized meal options. We begin with hearty hot meals that are light yet comforting, and then go onto raw salads that are perfect for light lunches and those warm summer evenings, and finish off with light and delicious fruit based desserts.

Introduction

When you switch to the vegan diet, you may be worried about whether or not you will still be able to eat your favorite foods. While you might have to make some big changes to your diet, there are plenty of vegan alternatives out there for traditional foods. You can still enjoy things like raw salads, noodles, stews, and entrees – even decadent desserts! The vegan diet is an excellent choice if you are looking for a way to improve your health and vitality and, with the recipes included in this book, you won't feel like you are making a sacrifice.

Another diet that has recently skyrocketed in popularity is the gluten-free diet. While many people are forced to switch to this diet out of medical necessity resulting from gluten allergies or intolerance, some people are making the switch simply because they think it is a healthy alternative to the modern Western diet.

The truth of the matter is that the gluten-free diet is not a magical solution for weight loss or health problems, but you can use it as a tool to achieve your health and wellness goals.

Health benefits of eating spiralized vegetables.

Eating spiralized food can help prevent heart attacks and heart diseases. Food rich in high sodium (Standard American Diet is full of processed foods... so SAD!) increases your blood pressure, so it's good to replace them with vegetables, which will make your body healthy and fit. Eating more nutrient-dense vegetables, rich in minerals and vitamins, while eliminating processed food (full of sugar, processed carbs, calories and chemicals), at the same time, helps in weight loss.

Spiralized food also helps in detoxing your body. Most spiralized vegetables, such as Zucchini, have plenty of water and help you stay hydrated and healthy. Most vegetables are full of fiber, and it's easier to digest them when you eat them in spiralized and slightly cooked form.

Veggies help stimulate your metabolism. You feel more energized! With a faster metabolism, your body performs efficiently to release the energy needed to get going. Metabolism improves absorption of nutrients, blood circulation, and digestion.

Spiralized vegetables are good for everyone! They can be of most help to those who have autoimmune diseases. It is because they are gluten free, natural and rich in nutrients.

Vegetable slicers are very useful for people who love cooking or want to cook in a healthier and more decorative style with convenience. Throughout the years, the number of vegetable slicers available on the market has continued to grow. It's mostly due to fact that there are more and more people who see the importance of having them in the kitchen and more and more people who want to eat a healthy diet.

Cooking can take a lot of time, and if you're a fan of vegetables, having a vegetable slicer may change your good kitchen experience into a great kitchen experience. Cutting vegetables can be a time consuming job, and you should have an appliance that will help make the preparation process a whole lot easier for you.

Regardless of which recipe you choose, do not be afraid to be creative and add or take away things, according to taste. Take what you like and reject the rest.

Hot Spiralized Meals

Inspired by cuisine from all over the world, these hot, comforting meals are light, healthy and sure to satisfy on even the coldest of winter nights. By using the Spiralizer these recipes will show you how you can still have your noodles, curries and pastas, only without the heavy gluten-based grains that are usually such a big part of such dishes. The inclusion of healthy fats and oils as well as fresh and dried herbs not only provide great flavor, but add to the nutritional benefits of the dishes. Non-animal proteins such as beans, lentils and tofu make these recipes even more satisfying without the added risk of consuming the cancer-causing antibiotics that farmed animals are fed.

Thai Noodles with Tofu
(Serves Two)

This tasty Thai-inspired dish uses potato noodles as opposed to the traditional rice noodles that are usually used. The tofu adds a good dose of protein and the crushed peanuts give the dish a distinct flavor.

Ingredients:

- 2 Cups (500ml) Firm tofu, diced
- 1 Large potato, Spiralized into noodles
- ½ Cup (125ml) Fresh bean sprouts
- 3 Spring onions, finely chopped
- 1 clove fresh garlic, finely chopped
- 2 teaspoons (10ml) fresh ginger root, finely chopped
- 1 small red onion, finely chopped
- 1 Tablespoon (15ml) fresh coriander, finely chopped
- 1 Tablespoon (15ml) crushed raw peanuts
- 1 Small fresh lime, quartered
- 2 Tablespoons (30ml) peanut oil

Instructions:

1. In a wok heat up 1 tablespoon (15ml) of the peanut oil and fry up the tofu until golden brown. Set aside.

2. Add the remaining tablespoon (15ml) of the peanut oil to the wok and fry up the spring onion, red onion, garlic and ginger root until soft.

3. Add the potato noodles and fresh coriander and fry until the potato has browned.

4. Add the bean sprouts and continue to stir fry for about 5 minutes, making sure to keep the crunch of the bean sprouts.

5. Remove from the heat and toss in the tofu.

6. Divide into two serving bowls and sprinkle each bowl with the crushed peanuts, and two quarters of the fresh lime. Squeeze the lime juice over the dish as per your personal preference.

Curried Roast Butternut Noodles and Chickpeas with Quinoa
(Serves 4)

Quinoa is a naturally gluten free grain that is high in vitamins, minerals, amino acids and proteins. It is so nutritious that it could very well be considered a super food. Chickpeas are also a healthy, high fiber protein source and the butternut provides potassium and vitamin B6. The mild curry flavor of this dish makes it a very comforting and heart-warming meal on a cold winter night.

Ingredients:

- 4 Cups (1litre) Spiralized Butternut
- 2 Cups (500ml) Cooked Quinoa
- 1 Can of chickpeas, drained and rinsed
- 2 Tablespoons (30ml) Peach Chutney
- 1 teaspoon (5ml) Masala curry mix
- ½ teaspoon (2.5ml) Ground cinnamon
- ¼ teaspoon (1.25ml) Cumin seeds
- 1 teaspoon (5ml) freshly chopped garlic
- 1 teaspoon (5ml) fresh ginger root, finely chopped
- 1 medium sized onion, finely chopped
- 4 teaspoons (20ml) Tahini

Instructions:

1. Heat the oven to 350 degrees (200degrees Celsius).

2. Spray an ovenproof dish with vegan friendly cooking spray.

3. Place the Spiralized butternut noodles, chickpeas, fresh garlic, ginger, chopped onion, Masala mix, and ground cinnamon in the baking dish. Add the peach chutney and stir all the ingredients together, making sure that all the ingredients are well coated with the chutney and spices.

4. Cook for about 45 minutes to an hour, or until the butternut noodles and the chickpeas are soft, and the sugars from the chutney have begun to caramelize over the ingredients. You want the butternut noodles and chickpeas to be soft as opposed to crunchy, so keep an eye on it so that it doesn't over-cook.

5. In four separate serving bowls, place ½ cup (125ml) quinoa in each bowl.

6. Top each bowl with the roasted butternut noodles and chickpeas.

7. Pour 1 teaspoon (5ml) of Tahini over each bowl and serve hot immediately.

Napolitano Zucchini Pasta with Red Kidney Beans
(Serves 4)

This is a low calorie take on the usual high carbohydrate based pasta dish. Tomatoes are high in vitamin C and essential minerals. Not only do the zucchinis add an extra dose of healthy fiber, but they are also high in vitamin C and essential minerals. The red kidney beans provide a good, wholesome, high fiber source of protein, making this dish a well-rounded nutritious gut-friendly meal. The extra virgin olive oil brings out the cancer-fighting properties of the tomatoes and together with the black olives, provides a healthy dose of essential fats.

Ingredients:

- 4 Cups (1litre) Spiralized zucchini
- 2 Cups (500ml) chopped fresh tomatoes
- 1 Can red kidney beans, drained and rinsed
- ½ Cup (125ml) black olives, pitted
- 1 teaspoon (5ml) freshly chopped garlic
- 1 large onion, finely chopped
- ½ teaspoon (2.5ml) ground black pepper
- ½ teaspoon (2,5ml) ground organic sea salt

- 1 teaspoon (5ml) mixed dried Italian herbs
- 1 Tablespoon (15ml) Extra Virgin Olive oil
- 1 Tablespoon (15ml) Fresh basil leaves, finely chopped

Instructions:

1. In a large saucepan, heat the extra virgin olive oil and fry the garlic and onion until it is transparent.
2. Add the chopped fresh tomatoes, red kidney beans, black olives, black pepper, sea salt and dried herbs. Bring to a simmer and allow cooking for about 20 minutes.
3. Add the zucchini noodles and allow cooking for a further ten minutes.
4. Divide into four serving bowls and garnish with the fresh basil leaves before serving.

Tomato and Eggplant with Carrot Noodles and Chickpeas
(Serves 4)

This is another take on the Napolitano tomato base pasta sauce. This recipe includes the vitamin A from the carrots and gets its protein form the chickpeas. The eggplant brings in a distinct flavor and once again the healthy fats are in the form of extra virgin olive oil and black olives.

Ingredients:

- 4 Cups (1litre) Spiralized carrots
- 2 Cups (500ml) Chopped fresh tomatoes
- 1 Can chick peas, drained and rinsed
- 1 large eggplant, diced
- ½ Cup (125ml) black olives, pitted
- 1 teaspoon (5ml) freshly chopped garlic
- 1 large onion, finely chopped
- ½ teaspoon (2.5ml) ground black pepper
- ½ teaspoon (2,5ml) ground organic sea salt
- 1 teaspoon (5ml) mixed dried Italian herbs
- 1 Tablespoon (15ml) Extra Virgin Olive oil
- 1 Tablespoon (15ml) Fresh basil leaves, finely chopped

Instructions:

1. In a large saucepan, heat the extra virgin olive oil and fry the garlic and onion until it is transparent.
2. Add the chopped fresh tomatoes, chickpeas, diced eggplant, black olives, black pepper, sea salt and dried herbs. Bring to a simmer and allow cooking for about 20 minutes.
3. Add the carrot noodles and allow cooking for a further ten minutes.
4. Divide into four serving bowls and garnish with the fresh basil leaves before serving.

Beetroot Noodles with Tofu, Brown Rice and Avocado
(Serves 4)

Although it is rather high in natural sugars, beetroot is known of its high vitamin C content as well as its cancer fighting properties. Brown rice is another healthy, high fiber gluten free grain that is high in B vitamins and essential minerals. Note: *Brown rice is naturally gluten-free, but in some cases, gluten can come into contact with brown rice. Be sure you choose 100% gluten-free options. If Celiac and not too sure about the brand- better skip this ingredient or use quinoa instead.*

The avocado oil and avocado provides the healthy fats in this recipe, while the tofu brings protein to the party.

Ingredients:

- 4 Cups (1litre) Spiralized beetroot
- 4 Cups (1litre) Firm Tofu
- 2 Cups (500ml) Cooked Brown rice
- 2 Tablespoons (30ml) Avocado oil
- 1 teaspoon (5ml) freshly chopped garlic

- 1 teaspoon (5ml) dried Italian herb mix
- ½ teaspoon (2.5ml) ground black pepper
- ½ teaspoon (2.5ml) ground organic sea salt
- 1 medium sized avocado for serving

Instructions:

1. Preheat the oven to 350degrees (200degres Celsius)
2. Pour one tablespoon (25ml) of the avocado oil onto a piece of kitchen towel and rub it over the ovenproof dish so as to well grease it.
3. Place the Spiralized beetroot noodles into the oven proof dish and toss around so that they can absorb some of the avocado oil.
4. Roast for 15 minutes
5. In a wok, heat up the remaining tablespoon (15ml) of avocado oil and fry up the chopped garlic with the black pepper, sea salt and dried herbs.
6. Add the tofu to the wok and fry until it is golden brown.
7. In four separate serving bowls place ½ cup (125ml) of the cooked brown rice into each bowl.
8. Divide the roasted beetroot noodles evenly over the four bowls of brown rice.
9. Top each bowl with an even amount of the stir-fried tofu

10. Divide the avocado into quarters and slice each quarter into thin slices. Garnish each bowl with the avocado and an extra grinding of black pepper.

Creamy Tofu with Sweet Potato Noodles and Cashew Nuts
(Serves 4)

Sweet potatoes are an excellent source of vitamin A and essential minerals. The coconut cream in this recipe adds a good dose of healthy fats, and the raw cashew nuts not only provide a nutty crunch, but are also high in essential fats and minerals. This recipe is a healthy, alternative to creamy, heavy pasta dishes.

Ingredients:

- 4 Cups (1litre) Spiralized Sweet potato
- 4 Cups (1litre) Firm tofu
- 2 Cups (500ml) Coconut Cream
- 2 Tablespoons (30ml) Coconut oil
- 4 Teaspoons (20ml) Desiccated Coconut
- 4 Teaspoons (20ml) Raw Cashew nuts, finely chopped

Instructions:

1. Preheat the oven to 350degrees (200degrees Celsius)
2. Pour one tablespoon (15ml) of the coconut oil over a piece of kitchen towel and rub the kitchen towel over and ovenproof dish in order to grease it.
3. Place the Spiralized sweet potato noodles in the oven proof dish and toss them around so as to absorb some of the coconut oil.
4. Roast for 15 to 20 minutes
5. In a wok heat up the remaining tablespoon (15ml) of coconut oil and fry the tofu until golden brown.
6. Add the desiccated coconut to the wok and stir fry with the tofu for a further 5 minutes.
7. Add the coconut cream to the wok and bring up to a simmer for a further 5 minutes.
8. In four separate serving bowls, divide the sweet potato noodles evenly among the bowls.
9. Top each bowl of noodles with an even amount of the tofu and coconut cream mixture.
10. Sprinkle 1 teaspoon (5ml) of the chopped cashew nuts over each bowl and serve.

Raw Spiralized Salads

These raw salad recipes include a variety of vegetables, fruits, nuts and seeds, as well some gluten free grains, making them well-rounded, nutritious, high fiber meals. The additions of home-made dressings in some instances provide tasty, healthier options over the commercially made dressings.

These recipes are perfect for a summer afternoon lunch or those warmer evenings out on the patio.

Cucumber, Mint and Chickpea Salad, with Home-made Lemon Dressing
(Serves 4)

Cucumbers are a great source of vitamin K, along with essential minerals. They are also known for their high water content, making them a great addition to any meal on a very hot day, as they will help ward of dehydration. Mint is known for its ability to aid digestion and the lemon dressing adds a little extra vitamin C. This recipe gets its protein from the chick peas.

Ingredients for the Salad:

- 4 Cups (1litre) Spiralized fresh cucumber
- 1 tin Chick Peas, drained and rinsed
- ½ cup (125ml) Fresh mint leaves, finely chopped

Ingredients for the Dressing:

- ¼ Cup (60ml) Avocado Oil
- 1 teaspoon (5ml) Agave Nectar
- ½ Cup (125ml) Freshly squeezed lemon juice

- 1 Tablespoon (15ml) lemon rind, finely grated

Instructions to make the salad:

1. In four separate serving bowls, place 1 cup (250ml) of the Spiralized cucumber
2. To each bowl add ½ Cup (125ml) of the chickpeas
3. Divide the chopped mint leaves evenly over each salad bowl

Instructions to make the dressing:

1. Pour the avocado oil into a large jug
2. Add the lemon zest, Agave nectar and the freshly squeezed lemon juice
3. Whisk all the ingredients together, making sure they are well mixed
4. Pour as much dressing as to your personal liking over each salad bowl just before serving.

Buckwheat and Beetroot Salad with Chia Seeds and Mustard Leaves
(Serves 4)

Buckwheat is another high fiber, gluten-free grain option that provides and nutty flavor to this salad. Chia seeds are considered a super food with their high omega 3 content, and the mustard leaves bring a hint of mustardy flavor to this delicious combination. This recipe gets its protein from the high fiber lentils.

Ingredients:

- 4 Cups (1litre) Spiralized Raw Beetroot
- 2 Cups (500ml) Cooked buckwheat
- 1 Can lentils, drained and rinsed
- 4 Tablespoons (60ml) Chia seeds
- 4 Tablespoons (60ml) Mustard leaves
- Ground black pepper and sea salt

Instructions:

1. In four separate serving bowls place ½ cup (125ml) of the cooked buckwheat and top each with ¼ cup (60ml) of the lentils

2. Top each bowl of buckwheat with 1 cup (250ml) of the Spiralized raw beetroot

3. Sprinkle 1 tablespoon (15ml) of the mustard leaves over each bowl,

4. Sprinkle 1 tablespoon (15ml) of Chia seeds over each bowl

5. Add ground black pepper and sea salt to taste before tossing all together and serving.

Spiralized Waldorf salad
(Serves 4)

This version of a traditional favorite uses the Spiralizer to give the ingredients and new look and feel. What further sets this recipe apart from the normal Waldorf salad is that it uses Tahini as a dressing as opposed to mayonnaise, and includes dried pineapple pieces instead of raisins. The inclusion of barley grass adds essential amino acids to the dish, as well as giving it a distinct flavor.

Ingredients:

- 4 Cups (1litre) Spiralized fresh red cabbage
- 2 Cups (500ml) Spiralized green apple, preferably Granny Smith apples
- 4 Tablespoons (60ml) Barley grass, chopped
- 4 Tablespoons (60ml) dried pineapple pieces
- 4 Tablespoons (60ml) Raw pecan nuts, roughly chopped
- 4 Tablespoons (60ml) Tahini

Instructions:

1. In four separate serving bowls, place 1 cup (250ml) of the raw Spiralized cabbage

2. Top each bowl of cabbage with ½ cup (125ml) of the Spiralized apple

3. To each bowl add 1 tablespoon (15ml) of the dried pineapple pieces

4. To each bowl add 1 tablespoon (15ml) of the chopped pecan nuts

5. To each bowl add 1 tablespoon (15ml) Barley grass

6. Top each bowl with 1 tablespoon (15ml) of Tahini and toss together before serving

Spiralized Carrot Salad with Quinoa, Tofu and Onion Relish
(Serves 4)

This recipe includes a delicious homemade onion relish that is versatile and very tasty at the same time. It does need to be made in advance though. The addition of mixed seeds adds a little extra crunch along with some healthy fats. Tofu is an incredibly versatile protein source, since, as this recipe proves, it can be enjoyed cold as well as hot. Tofu does need to be cooked first as well.

Ingredients for the salad:

- 2 Cups (500ml) cooked quinoa
- 4 Cups (1litre) Spiralized raw carrot
- 2 Cups (500ml) Homemade onion relish
- 4 Cups (1litre) Cooked firm tofu
- 4 Tablespoons (60ml) Mixed raw seeds

Ingredients for the onion relish:

- 10 Medium sized white onions, peeled, halved and sliced
- 2 Tablespoons (30ml) Raw brown sugar
- 1 Cup (250ml) Balsamic Vinegar
- 2 Cloves of garlic, finely chopped
- Ground black pepper and salt to taste

Instructions to make the Onion Relish:

1. Preheat the oven to 350 degrees (200degrees Celsius)
2. Grease a large roasting pan with some extra virgin olive oil
3. Place the sliced onions, chopped garlic, brown sugar, salt, pepper and balsamic vinegar into the roasting pan and mix well.
4. Roast in the oven until the onions have completely softened and all the balsamic vinegar has evaporated
5. Place in a glass mason jar, while still hot. Seal the jar tightly and turn it upside down to cool, this will create a vacuum in the jar that will help preserve the onion relish.
6. Once the jar has been opened, store in the refrigerator.

Instructions to make the salad:

1. In four separate serving bowls place ½ Cup (125ml) of the cooked quinoa
2. Top each bowl of quinoa with 1 cup (250ml) of the Spiralized raw carrot
3. To each bowl add 1 cup (250ml) of the cooked tofu
4. Top each bowl with ½ cup (125ml) of the onion relish
5. Just before serving sprinkle 1 tablespoon (15ml) of the mixed raw seeds over each bowl.

Raw Zucchini, Spinach, Tomato and Black Olive Salad with Homemade Balsamic Dressing
(Serves 4)

This salad has a great flavor combination and is packed with health benefits from the raw vegetables, and healthy fats from both the black olives and the homemade balsamic dressing.

Ingredients to make the salad:

- 4 cups (1litre) Spiralized raw zucchini
- 2 Cups (500ml) Raw spinach, finely chopped
- 4 Tablespoons (60ml) Fresh basil leaves, finely chopped
- 2 Cups (500ml) Cherry tomatoes, halved
- 4 Tablespoons (60ml) Black olives, pitted

Ingredients to make the dressing:

- 1 cup (250ml) Extra virgin olive oil
- ½ cup (125ml) Balsamic vinegar
- 1 teaspoon (5ml) Dried Italian herb mix

- ½ teaspoon (2.5ml) Ground black pepper
- ½ teaspoon (2.5ml) Ground organic sea salt

Instructions to make the dressing:

1. Pour the extra virgin olive oil and balsamic vinegar into a salad dressing shaker.
2. Add the herbs, salt and pepper and shake well to mix
3. The oil and vinegar will separate while standing so you will need to give it another shake before use.

Instructions to make the salad:

1. In four separate serving bowls place 1 cup (250ml) of the Spiralized raw zucchini
2. To each bowl add ½ cup (125ml) Raw chopped spinach
3. To each bowl add 1 tablespoon (15ml) of the chopped basil leaves
4. To each bowl add ½ cup (125ml) of the cherry tomatoes
5. To each bowl add 1 tablespoon (15ml) of the black olives
6. Just before serving add dressing to taste and toss well.

Note on balsamic vinegar:

There's a very small possibility that balsamic vinegar could be contaminated with wheat or rye flour but only those most sensitive to trace gluten would notice (far less than 1% of everyone who reacts to gluten). Otherwise, balsamic vinegar should be safe on the gluten-free diet. If you are not too sure about your balsamic vinegar brand, use apple cider vinegar or cane vinegar instead.

Spiralized Broccoli, Green Bean and Red Kidney Bean Salad with Onion Relish and Chia Seeds
(Serves 4)

Broccoli is a great source of fiber and calcium. Green beans are packed with essential vitamins and minerals, and they add a little sweetness to the overall flavor of this salad. The red kidney beans add some more fiber and protein to this recipe. The flavor is enhanced by the onion relish and the Chia seeds add some super food value.

Ingredients:

- 4 Cups (1litre) Spiralized raw broccoli
- 2 Cups (500ml) Spiralized raw green beans
- 1 Can Red kidney beans, drained and rinsed
- 2 Cups (500ml) Homemade Onion Relish (see recipe on page 13)
- 4 Tablespoons (60ml) Chia Seeds

Instructions:

1. In four separate serving bowls, place 1 cup (250ml) of the Spiralized raw broccoli
2. To each bowl add ½ cup (125ml) of the Spiralized raw green beans
3. To each bowl add ¼ cup (60ml) of the red kidney beans
4. Top each bowl with ½ cup (125ml) of the onion relish
5. Before serving sprinkle 1 tablespoon (15ml) of Chia seeds over each bowl

Spiralized Butternut, Buckwheat and Chickpea Salad
(Serves 4)

This wholesome salad is very filling and high in fiber. The added flavor from the fresh coriander seems to compliment that of the curry spices and chutney in the dressing. With the extra natural sweetness of the butternut and the golden sultanas, you'll wonder if you're not actually eating dessert.

Ingredients for the salad:

- 2 Cups (500ml) Cooked buckwheat
- 4 Cups (1litre) Raw Spiralized butternut
- 1 Can chickpeas, drained and rinsed
- 4 Tablespoons (60ml) Fresh coriander, finely chopped
- 4 Tablespoons (60ml) Raw Sesame seeds
- 4 Tablespoons (60ml) Golden Sultanas

Ingredients for the dressing:

- ¼ cup (60ml) Peach chutney

- 1 teaspoon (5ml) Masala curry mix
- ¼ teaspoon (1.25ml) Ground cinnamon
- 2 Tablespoons (30ml) Wine vinegar

Instructions to make the dressing:

1. Place the peach chutney and the wine vinegar into a jug.
2. Add the Masala mix and the ground cinnamon.
3. Whisk together until all is mixed well.

Instructions to make the salad:

1. In four separate serving bowls, place ½ cup (250ml) of the cooked buckwheat
2. To each bowl add 1 cup (250ml) of the raw Spiralized butternut
3. To each bowl add ¼ cup (60ml) of the chickpeas
4. To each bowl add 1 tablespoon (15ml) of the fresh coriander
5. To each bowl add 1 tablespoon (15ml) of the golden sultanas
6. Top each bowl with the amount of dressing you desire and toss together

7. Before serving sprinkle 1 tablespoon (15ml) of the sesame seeds over each bowl.

Eggplant, Tomato and Black Bean Salad with Homemade Onion Relish
(Serves 4)

Even though this section is about recipes based on raw vegetables, there are some vegetables that really are not palatable raw, eggplant is one of them, so this recipe requires a little pre-preparation in the form of cooking the eggplant.

To prepare the Eggplant:

1. If your Spiralizer has a slicing option set it to that, otherwise slice 4 medium sized eggplants into thin slices.
2. Spray non-stick baking sheets (you may need more than one) with vegan friendly cooking spray and place the eggplant slices onto the baking sheets.
3. Preheat the oven to 300 degrees (200 degrees Celsius)
4. Cook the eggplant slices for twenty minutes, once cooked allow them to cool.

Ingredients for the Salad:

- 4 Cups (1litre) Cooked eggplant
- 2 Cups (500ml) Raw cherry tomatoes, halved
- 2 Cups (500ml) Homemade onion relish (see recipe on page 13)
- 1 Can black beans, drained and rinsed
- 4 Tablespoons (60ml) fresh basil, chopped
- 4 Tablespoons (60ml) black olives, pitted

Instructions:

1. In four separate serving bowls, place 1 cup (250ml) of the cooked eggplant
2. To each bowl add ½ cup (125ml) of the cherry tomatoes
3. To each bowl add ¼ cup (60ml) of the black beans
4. To each bowl add 1 tablespoon (15ml) of the fresh basil leaves
5. To each bowl add 1 tablespoon (15ml) of the black olives
6. Top each bowl with ½ cup (125ml) onion relish
7. Toss together and serve

Spiralized Fruity Desserts

Everyone loves dessert, but just because you're focused on being healthy, doesn't mean you have to skip it. The recipes in this section use the Spiralizer device to create healthy, fresh fruit based desserts that will nourish your body by providing you with essential vitamins, minerals and healthy fats.

Spiralized Pineapple, Cashew Nut and Coconut Dessert
(Serves 4)

Pineapples are loaded with essential vitamins and minerals and the cashew nuts, Tahini and coconut add a good dose of heart healthy fats. With its tropical feel, this dessert would be a great end to a meal including the **Curried Roast Butternut Noodles and Chickpeas with Quinoa,** found on page 3.

Ingredients:

- 4 Cups (1litre) Spiralized fresh pineapple
- 2 cups (250ml) Spiralized fresh coconut
- 4 Tablespoons (60ml) Raw cashew nuts, roughly chopped
- 4 Tablespoons (60ml) Tahini (should say gluten-free on the label)

Instructions:

1. In four separate serving bowls, place 1 cup (250ml) of the fresh Spiralized pineapple
2. To each bowl add ½ cup (125ml) of the fresh Spiralized coconut
3. To each bowl add 1 tablespoon (15ml) of the raw chopped cashew nuts
4. Before serving pour 1 tablespoon (15ml) of the Tahini over each bowl.

Spiralized Pear, Grape and Chocolaty Almond Dessert
(Serves 4)

Pears are another great source of vitamin C, grapes are also highly nutritious and add natural sweetness to anything you put them with, and almonds are not only tasty, but give a good dose of vitamin E. The chocolaty, almond milk sauce adds a little comfort without the high calories of normal chocolate sauces, and its raw cocoa content makes it high in anti-oxidants.

Ingredients for the dessert:

- 4 Cups (1litre) Spiralized fresh pear
- 2 Cups (500ml) Fresh red grapes, halved (red in particular because they add a little color)
- 4 Tablespoons (40ml) Raw almonds, chopped

Ingredients for the chocolate sauce:

- 1 cup (250ml) Almond Milk
- 1 teaspoon (5ml) Raw cocoa powder
- ¼ teaspoon (2.5ml) Ground cinnamon
- 1 tablespoon (15ml) Almond essence
- 1 teaspoon (5ml) Vanilla essence

Instructions to make the chocolate sauce:

1. Pour the almond milk into the jug of a blender
2. Add the cocoa powder, ground cinnamon, almond and vanilla essence
3. Blend together until well mixed

Instructions to make the dessert:

1. In four separate serving bowls, place 1 cup (250ml) of the fresh Spiralized pear
2. To each bowl add ½ cup (125ml) of the red grapes
3. To each bowl add 1 tablespoon (15ml) of the chopped raw almonds

4. Before serving pour ¼ cup (60ml) of the chocolate
   almond sauce over each bowl.

Spiralized Apple, Ginger, Berry and Brazil nut Dessert with Coconut Cream
(Serves 4)

Apples are high in vitamins, minerals, fiber and anti-oxidants. Ginger is well known for its immune-boosting and anti-inflammatory properties. The dried berry mix, with its inclusion of super food Goji berries, cranberries and cherries, add extra anti-oxidants to the recipe. Brazil nuts bring essential selenium to the mix and the coconut cream not only adds a creamy taste, but also essential fats. It would be best to make this dessert just before serving so that the apple does not brown.

Ingredients:

- 4 Cups (1litre) Spiralized fresh apple, it's a nice idea to mix red and green apples to add variety to the flavor and color. It's also preferable not to peel the apples, as this will add extra fiber and avoid the loss of the essential nutrients that lie just under the skin of the fruit.
- 1 Cup (250ml) Dried berry mix
- 4 Tablespoons (60ml) Fresh ginger root, finely chopped
- 4 Tablespoons (60ml) Raw Brazil nuts, finely chopped
- 1 cup (250ml) Coconut Cream

Instructions:

1. In four separate serving bowls, place 1 cup (250ml) of the Spiralized apple

2. To each bowl add 1 tablespoon (15ml) of the fresh ginger root

3. To each bowl add ¼ cup (60ml) of the dried berry mix

4. To each bowl add 1 tablespoon (15ml) of the chopped raw brazil nuts

5. Just before serving pour ¼ cup (60ml) of the coconut cream over each bowl.

Spiralized Peach, Nectarine and Hazelnut Dessert with a Chocolaty Twist
(Serves 4)

Peaches and nectarines are another great source of essential vitamins, minerals and anti-oxidants. Hazelnuts are also high in fiber, essential vitamins, minerals and healthy fats, and their flavor really compliments that of the raw cocoa nibs, which, like raw cocoa powder, is a super food, high in anti-oxidants.

Ingredients:

- 4 Cups (1litre) Equal quantities of Spiralized peaches and nectarines
- 4 Tablespoons (60ml) Raw hazelnuts, roughly chopped
- 4 Tablespoons (60ml) Raw cocoa nibs
- 1 Cup (250ml) Plain dairy-free, gluten-free yoghurt
- 1 teaspoon (5ml) Vanilla essence

Instructions:

1. In four separate serving bowls, place 1 cup (250ml) of the Spiralized peach and nectarine combination
2. To each bowl add 1 tablespoon (15ml) of the chopped hazelnuts
3. To each bowl add 1 tablespoon (15ml) of the raw cocoa nibs
4. In a separate bowl mix the yoghurt with the vanilla essence
5. Before serving top each serving bowl with ¼ cup (60ml) of the yoghurt.

Spiralized Papaya, Sultana, Pistachio and Coconut Dessert
(Serves 4)

Papayas are another great source of essential vitamins and minerals. The sultanas add as chewy texture to this combination while the slight saltiness of the pistachios brings a contrast to the sweetness of the papaya. The coconut adds some healthy fats and a little tropical flavor.

Ingredients:

- 4 Cups (1litre) Spiralized fresh papaya
- 2 Cups (250ml) Spiralized fresh coconut
- 1 Cup (250ml) Golden Sultanas
- 4 Tablespoons (60ml) Raw pistachios, roughly chopped

Instructions:

1. In four separate serving bowls, place 1 cup (250ml) of the Spiralized fresh papaya
2. To each bowl add ½ cup (125ml) of the Spiralized fresh coconut
3. To each bowl add ¼ cup (60ml) of the golden sultanas
4. Top each bowl with 1 tablespoon (15ml) of the chopped pistachios, and serve.

Spiralized Banana, Berry and Pecan nut Dessert with Chocolaty Yoghurt
(Serves 4)

Bananas could be called a super food as they are packed with so many essential vitamins, minerals and amino acids, they are a staple in any sportsperson's kitchen and their numerous health benefits make them an essential part of any diet. Dairy-free yoghurt (for example almond milk yoghurt) is high in protein, and the pecan nuts bring along some extra essential minerals as well as their healthy fats. Extra anti- oxidants come in the addition of super foods such as the raw cocoa and the dried berry mix that contains Goji berries. This dessert would actually be perfect for any sportsperson the night before an event. It will be best to prepare this dessert just before serving so that the banana does not go brown.

Ingredients:

- 4 cups (1litre) Spiralized bananas, it's essential to make sure that the bananas are not too ripe, rather a little green, otherwise they may turn to mush when you put them through your Spiralizer.
- 2 cups (500ml) Dried berry mix

- 4 Tablespoons (60ml) Raw pecan nuts, chopped
- 1 cup (250ml) dairy-free gluten-free yoghurt
- 1 teaspoon (5ml) Raw cocoa powder
- ¼ teaspoon (1.25ml) ground cinnamon
- ½ teaspoon (2.5ml) vanilla essence

Instructions:

1. In four separate serving bowls, place 1 cup (250ml) of the Spiralized banana
2. To each bowl add ½ cup (125ml) of the dried berry mix
3. To each bowl add 1 tablespoon (25ml) of the chopped pecan nuts
4. In a separate bowl, mix the yoghurt, raw cocoa powder, ground cinnamon and vanilla essence
5. Before serving, top each bowl with ¼ cup (60ml) of the yoghurt mix.

Spiralized Apple and Cinnamon Dessert
(Serves 4)

This comforting dessert can't but help remind one of a good old apple pie! Only this one doesn't come with the added unnecessary calories, and since the apple is raw, it still has all its nutritional value completely intact. The addition of spices such as cinnamon and cloves make this dessert a wonderful way to end a winter's night. This is another of those desserts that is best prepared just before serving so as to ensure that the apple doesn't brown.

Ingredients:

- 4 Cups (1litre) Spiralized fresh apples, again it's a nice idea to have a mix of green and red apples, so as to add variety of flavor and color, and again it is recommended that you don't peel the apples.
- 2 Cups (500ml) Raisins
- 4 Tablespoons (60ml) Fresh ginger root, finely chopped
- 4 Tablespoons (60ml) Raw almonds, finely chopped
- 1 teaspoon (5ml) Ground cinnamon
- 1 teaspoon (5ml) Ground cloves
- 1 Cup (250ml) dairy-free gluten-free yoghurt
- 1 teaspoon (5ml) vanilla essence

Instructions:

1. In four separate serving bowls, place 1 cup (250ml) of the Spiralized fresh apple
2. To each bowl add ½ cup (125ml) of the raisins
3. To each bowl add 1 Tablespoon (15ml) of the fresh ginger
4. To each bowl add 1 Tablespoon (15ml) of the raw almonds
5. In a separate bowl, mix the yoghurt, ground cinnamon, ground cloves and vanilla essence.
6. Before serving top each bowl with ¼ cup (60ml) of the yoghurt mixture

Spiralized Fresh Pear, Fig, Date and Macadamia nut Dessert
(Serves 4)

Figs contain a reasonable amount of calcium, and like all fruits and vegetables provide essential vitamins and minerals, their potassium content makes them known for their ability to lower blood pressure. Dates are a great source of fiber and the essential mineral, iron; they also add a chewy sweetness to this recipe. Macadamia nuts are good source of vitamin A and protein.

Ingredients:

- 4 Cups (1litre) Spiralized fresh pear
- 2 Cups (500ml) fresh figs, halved
- 1 Cup (250ml) Dates, chopped
- 4 Tablespoons (60ml) Raw macadamia nuts, finely chopped
- 1 Cup (250ml) Dairy-free, gluten-free yoghurt
- 1 teaspoon (5ml) Vanilla essence

Instructions:

1. In four separate serving bowls, place 1 cup (250ml) of the Spiralized fresh pear
2. To each bowl add ½ cup (125ml) of the fresh figs
3. To each bowl add ¼ cup (60ml) of the chopped dates
4. To each bowl add 1 Tablespoon (15ml) of the chopped macadamia nuts
5. In a separate bowl, mix the yoghurt and the vanilla essence
6. Before serving, top each bowl with ¼ cup (60ml) of the yoghurt mixture.

Spiralized Mango, Coconut and Brazil nut Dessert, with dried Apricots
(Serves 4)

Mangoes are rich in pre-biotic dietary fiber, making them an excellent aid to promoting a healthy gut. They also contain essential vitamins and minerals. The flavor of the mangoes is complimented by the other ingredients in this dessert and the addition of the dried apricots provides a chewy sweetness and an extra dose of fiber.

Ingredients:

- 4 Cups (1litre) Spiralized fresh mango, it is recommended that the mangoes are not too ripe, as the firmer they are the easier it will be to put them through your Spiralizer device.
- 2 Cups (500ml) Spiralized fresh coconut
- 1 Cup (250ml) Dried apricots, chopped
- 4 Tablespoons (60ml) Raw Brazil nuts, roughly chopped
- 1 Cup (250ml) dairy-free gluten-free yoghurt
- 1 teaspoon (5ml) vanilla essence

Instructions:

1. In four separate serving bowls, place 1 Cup (250ml) of the Spiralized mango
2. To each bowl add ½ cup (125ml) of the Spiralized fresh coconut
3. To each bowl add ¼ cup (60ml) of the chopped dried apricots
4. To each bowl add 1 Tablespoon (15ml) of the chopped raw brazil nuts
5. In a separate bowl, mix the yoghurt and the vanilla essence
6. Before serving, top each bowl with ¼ cup (60ml) of the yoghurt mixture.

Before you go, I'd like to remind you that there is a free, complimentary eBook waiting for you. Download it today to treat yourself to healthy, <u>gluten-free desserts and snacks</u> so that you never feel deprived again!

Download link

<u>http://bit.ly/gluten-free-desserts-book</u>

Conclusion

While the gluten-free diet is a medical treatment for individuals with celiac disease or gluten intolerance, it can be beneficial for nearly everyone. Before you decide whether the gluten-free diet is the right choice for you, take the time to learn as much as you can about the diet including its benefits, its risks, and which foods you can and cannot eat. Check out my website for more information where you will find the food lists and recipes to get started:

http://www.kiraglutenfreerecipes.com

There are different kinds of gluten-free diets (for example Paleo, vegetarian, vegan). You don't have to go 100% vegan to enjoy a gluten-free diet as it can be personalized. It's totally up to you. However, I believe that we should all learn more vegan options and reduce the consumption of animal products. This does not have to be painful as there are many delicious, plant-based options out there.

My main focus, as an author, is to create helpful and information gluten-free and anti-inflammatory recipe books that can accommodate vegans, vegetarians and paleo diet enthusiasts.

Your Comments Are Important

One more thing... If you have received any value from this book, can you please rank it and post a short review? It only takes a few seconds really and it would really make my day. It's you I am writing for and your opinion is always much appreciated. In order to do so;

1. Log into your account
2. Search for my book on Amazon or check your orders/ or go to my author page at:

<u>http://amazon.com/author/kira-novac</u>

3. Click on a book you have read, then click on "reviews" and "create your review".

Please let me know your favorite recipe. I would love to hear from you!

If you happen to have any questions or doubts about this book, please e-mail me at:

kira.novac@kiraglutenfreerecipes.com

I am here to help!

Recommended Reading

Book Link:

http://bit.ly/vegan-gf-baking

Recommended Reading

Book Link:

http://bit.ly/gluten-free-vegan

FOR MORE HEALTH BOOKS (KINDLE & PAPERBACK) BY KIRA NOVAC PLEASE VISIT:

www.kiraglutenfreerecipes.com/books

Thank you for taking an interest in my work,

Kira and Holistic Wellness Books

HOLISTIC WELLNESS & HEALTH BOOKS

If you are interested in health, wellness, spirituality and personal development, visit our page and be the first one to know about free and 0.99 eBooks:

www.holisticwellnessbooks.com

Made in the USA
Lexington, KY
28 April 2016